One-Minute Meditations

For Communion and Offering

by Knofel Staton

Wipf and Stock Publishers
EUGENE, OREGON

Dedicated
to Him whom we honor
in the Communion
and whose kingdom we expand
in the offering.

Wipf and Stock Publishers
199 West 8th Avenue, Suite 3
Eugene, Oregon 97401

One Minute Meditations
By Staton, Knofel

ISBN: 1-57910-470-3
Publication date: September, 2000
Previously published by Standard Publishing, 1991.

Contents

Foreword

These one-minute meditations were written with these objectives in mind:

1. They will tie into the Biblical meaning and reason for Communion and offering.

2. They will connect to practical issues that we face today.

3. They will communicate and come to the point.

4. They will reflect the same idea as the Scripture texts and the prayers.

The index for each part links up the meditations to issues we face today as well as special days on the church calendar.

These meditations can be used in several ways:

1. One person can share all aspects of each meditation—that is, read the text, give the meditation, and offer the prayer.

2. One person can share the text,

meditation, and prayer for the Communion time and another person can share for the offering time.

3. Three different people could be used for the Communion—one for the text, one for the meditation, and one for the prayer.

4. Likewise, three different people could be used for the offering section.

5. Each meditation unit (text, meditation, and prayer) could be printed in the bulletin, in a bulletin insert, or on overhead transparencies for people to read. They could be read silently, read in unison, or read responsively—that is, the person presiding could read one part, while the congregation reads another.

Various members of the congregation could be used, such as elders, deacons, Sunday-school teachers, youth group members, senior saints, members of a family, members of the single's group, or any other group in your church. Show the unity and involvement of the body by using these combinations on occasion:

1. All the church staff could share one part in unison while the congregation responds.

2. The parents could share one part, while the children respond.

3. One Sunday-school class, sitting as a group, could share one part, while another class responds.

4. The choir could share one part, while the congregation responds.

5. The women could share one part, while the men respond.

6. The elders could share one part, while the deacons respond. The combinations are endless.

My hope is that these meditations will make a positive difference in the understanding, appreciation, participation, and application of the meaning of the Lord's Supper and the offering.

—Knofel Staton
Fullerton, California

Part 1: Communion Meditations

The Shepherd Became the Lamb

Scripture Reading

"I am the good shepherd. The good shepherd lays down his life for the sheep" (John 10:11).

Meditation

What a paradox! The Good Shepherd became the sacrificial lamb. His whole life was paradoxical. The Bread of Life hungered. The Living Water thirsted. The Rock was crushed. The King became a servant. He who is loved was hated. The Friend if sinners was rejected by sinners. The Healer was wounded. The Merciful was treated without mercy. The Forgiver was charged falsley. The Truth was lied against. The Creator was crucified on a tree. The Eternal One died, but He died in our place. He arose never to die again. In Him we will pass from death into life.

Prayer

Some are here today, Father, who hurt because of the death of a loved one. Some are here who feel uncertain because the doctor has told them their illness is terminal. We are reluctant to think about death, but remind us, Father, that death for us is just a doorway to life with You through Jesus Christ. Amen.

Nobody Is a Nobody

Scripture Reading

"Because there is one loaf, we, who are many, are one body, for we all partake of the one loaf" (1 Corinthians 10:17).

Meditation

The one loaf reminds us of Christ's body in the first century and His continual body —the church. As the one body of Christ existed on earth then, so only one body of Christ still exists on earth now. One of the benefits of Christ's death for us is that in Him we are added to His ongoing body—the church. As we look around, we may sometimes feel either inferior or superior to one another, but the cross reminds us that we came into Christ at the same level—sinners in need of forgiveness. And, as members of that body, we must remember that we need each other. Nobody is a nobody in Christ's body.

Prayer

Father, we consider Jesus during this Communion time, but He is not the only one to consider. Help us to do as He did—

think of others and commit ourselves to serve them in love. Amen.

Partners Together

Scripture Reading

"Is not the cup of thanksgiving for which we give thanks a participation in the blood of Christ? And is not the bread that we break a participation in the body of Christ?"(1 Corinthians 10:16).

Meditation

To *participate in* means *to become partners with*. In the partaking of the cup, we are committing ourselves to be living sacrifices for one another as Jesus' blood was sacrificed for us. By partaking of the bread we commit our bodies to help meet the needs of others. In the same way Christ's body met the needs of others in the first century.

Prayer

Father, forgive me for wanting Christianity to be just one way—You for me—instead of two ways—You for me and me for You. Because You instituted the Lord's Supper on the night You sacrificed yourself for others, may we desire the motivation to live for others as well this week. Amen.

Getting Along

Scripture Reading

"In the first place, I hear that when you come together as a church, there are divisions among you, and to some extent I believe it. . . . When you come together, it is not the Lord's Supper you eat, for as you eat, each of you goes ahead without waiting for anybody else" (1 Corinthians 11:18, 20, 21).

Meditation

The Lord's Supper reconciles our attitudes toward those with whom we have differences in God's family. Paul criticized people for partaking of the Lord's Supper when they had dissensions within the body. The Lord's Supper is to be a family meal—a meal of peace with God and with each other.

Prayer

Father, during this Communion time remind us that we not only have a Father but eternal brothers and sisters who are now sitting all around us. Help us to please You by treating Your other children with love. Amen.

Sensitive to Others

Scripture Reading

"When you come together, it is not the Lord's Supper you eat, for as you eat, each of you goes ahead without waiting for anybody else. One remains hungry, another gets drunk. Don't you have homes to eat and drink in? Or do you despise the church of God and humiliate those who have nothing?" (1 Corinthians 11:20-22).

Meditation

During the first century, the Lord's Supper was often taken as part of a bigger meal called the "agape meal." This pitch-in meal insured that the poor members of the body had something to eat. But some, not waiting for the poor to arrive, gorged themselves. They left nothing for the poor to eat. After the poor arrived, everyone would partake of the Lord's Supper as an evidence that they were united in Christ. How ironic that they could partake of a meal of unity without being sensitive to their brothers and sisters in serious need. The Lord's Supper reminds us that Jesus unites us, and we should show sensitivity to and responsibility for one another's needs.

Prayer

Father, it is so easy to think of ourselves

first, and often, only. During this time of Communion, flash across our minds those among us who have needs and motivate us to be open to reach out with the love of Christ. Amen.

A Death That Unites

Scripture Reading

"For whenever you eat this bread and drink this cup, you proclaim the Lord's death until he comes" (1 Corinthians 11:26).

Meditation

What is it that we proclaim about the Lord's death in the Communion service? We proclaim the historical fact that He died. And we also proclaim the purpose—that He died to unite mankind to himself and to one another. Just look around. The rich and the poor, the banker and the welfare recipient, the Ph.D. and the high school dropout, the well and the sick, male and female—they all make up this family because Jesus' death and resurrection unites men.

Prayer

Father, we who were once far off have been brought near to You through Jesus. Enable our hearts to be big enough to see others who are far off and invite and include them in the nearness of Your family. Amen.

Worth in the Family

Scripture Reading

"Therefore, whoever eats the bread or drinks the cup of the Lord in an unworthy manner will be guilty of sinning against the body and blood of the Lord" (1 Corinthians 11:27).

Meditation

Have you ever heard anyone say that "we are not worthy to partake of the Lord's Supper"? That's wrong. We are worthy because Christ died for us. We are the children of God. We are forgiven. We know that Christ is coming back for us. All of these reasons makes us worthy. While children can be worthy to have dinner with their parents at home, they can eat it in an unworthy manner. The unworthy manner mentioned in this passage of Scripture refers to an attitude. Fusses and fights with one another in the body exemplify action of alienation. Let's forgive, for we are all His.

Prayer

Thank You, Father, for seeing our worth

and adopting us, redeeming us, equipping us, using us—and coming back for us. Help us treat others as You would. Amen.

Sins Are Abolished

Scripture Reading

"This is my blood of the covenant, which is poured out for many for the forgiveness of sins" (Matthew 26:28).

Meditation

The Lord's Supper reminds us that our sins have been forgiven. The word *forgiveness* denotes complete release, deliverance, and dismissal. The root of the Greek word means *to send away*. When God forgives our sins, He does not remember them anymore. Shouldn't we put a "keep out" sign on our spirits so we can resist sin from entering into our inner selves? Shouldn't we put a "no fishing allowed" sign over our minds so we stop fishing for remembrances of our past sins or the sins of others? God has forgiven!

Prayer

It is so easy to live without forgetting—forgetting our sins. But we thank You, Father, that You know how to forget and that You remember to do it on a consistent basis. Amen.

God's Forgetfulness

Scripture Reading

"This is the blood of my covenant, which is poured out for many for the forgiveness of sins" (Matthew 26:28).

Meditation

Shouldn't we strive to remember what God remembers and to forget what God forgets? God promises to forget our sins. Too many times we keep mulling over our mistakes, remembering our sins, and feeling our guilt. But God has wiped our slate clean. The prophet Isaiah reminds that though our sins are like scarlet, they will be as white as snow. Though they are red as crimson, they shall be as wool.

The evangelist told Paul that his sins could be washed away. During this Communion time, allow God's grace to lighten your burdens and lift you up to see His mercy.

Prayer

No one is as blind as that person who cannot or will not see the good You have done, Father. You have cleaned us of our past. Help us not to not mentally crawl through the mud of our past anymore. In Christ's name, Amen.

Our History

Scripture Reading

"To him who loves us and has freed us from our sins by his blood, and has made us to be a kingdom and priests to serve his God and Father—to him be glory and power for ever and ever! Amen" (Revelation 1:5, 6).

Meditation

The Lord's Supper reminds us of our past and how our sins have been forgiven. It also reminds us of the present and how Jesus Christ is now with us. Our Savior promised, "I will be with you." The Lord's Supper also reminds us of our future and how He is coming again for us. Consequently, during the Lord's Supper we are reminded that our whole history belongs to Him—past, present, future. This is a time to recommit ourselves to Him for the rest of this day and for the tomorrows of our lives.

Prayer

Father, forgive us for the pride and arrogance that allows us to struggle through life without inviting You to be a part of it, as if we served an absentee God. Remind us during this time that without You we cannot live and without You we dare not die. Amen.

Future Assured

Scripture Reading

"I tell you, I will not drink of this fruit of the vine from now on until that day when I drink it anew with you in my Father's kingdom" (Matthew 26:29).

Meditation

The Lord's Supper reminds us that the Christian has a fantastic future. Jesus promised to eat this meal with us when He comes again. We belong to Him and are joint heirs with Him. Already we have an appointment to participate in a grand "marriage banquet" when Jesus comes again. He will come for his beautiful bride, the church. Then He will wipe away all tears. There will be no more pain or mourning or crying. The old order of things will have passed away. That will happen in "an hour when you think not."

Prayer

Father, thank You for inviting us to the wedding supper of the Lamb. We look forward to falling at Your feet and singing to You those grand words, "the kingdom of the world has become the kingdom of our Lord and of his Christ, and He will reign forever and ever." Amen.

It's Personal

Scripture Reading

"This is my body, which is for you" (1 Corinthians 11:24).

Meditation

Jesus' love is personal. "This is my body, which is for you." Notice the "for you." He had you in mind. God knows you by name. He even knows the number of hairs on your head. In spite of knowing you, it was "for you" that Christ gave himself. Change the pronoun "you" to your name. Hear Jesus say, "This is my body, which is for (**your name**)." Regardless of the circumstances you are now going through, Jesus loves you personally. If only you and Jesus lived in the world, He would still have died just for you. Somebody out there loves you—and that somebody is Jesus.

Prayer

We all want to be loved, but often we feel so unlovable. Thank You, Father, for giving Yourself in the person of Jesus and saying through Him, "You are precious in my sight, and I love you."

I Love You

Scripture Reading

"Since you are precious and honored in my sight, and because I love you . . ." (Isaiah 43:4).

Meditation

Nowhere do we see those words of God demonstrated to us better than in God's watching His Son die on the cross for us. God deems us valuable. Our self-esteem stems from this basis. The world talks us down, holds us down, and puts us down. Low self-esteem pervades our minds, but when we see Jesus on the cross, we see God's evaluation of us. In a sense, God said, "Your sinful self is worth my perfect Son."

With every new day that comes God says, "the world is worth continuing, and you are worth staying in it."

Prayer

Help us, God, to quit looking down and seeing just our mess. Help us to look up and see Your majesty and mercy and love and grace and peace in the sacrifice of Jesus. Amen.

You Are a Preacher

Scripture Reading

"For whenever you eat this bread and drink this cup, you proclaim the Lord's death until he comes" (1 Corinthians 11:26).

Meditation

As we participate in the Lord's Supper, we each become "preachers and proclaimers." We don't just proclaim that He died but also why He died. He died so that we could be reunited to God and to each other. He died so that we could look beyond the grave. He died so that we could become vessels of His Holy Spirit. He died so that our sins would not haunt us when He comes back. He died so that we would not run to the rocks and hills but run to praise Him the instant He returns.

Prayer

Bring us to the foot of the cross, Father, so that You can melt our hearts and break our arrogance. We know that we can be saved only by Your grace, not of our works. Thank You for giving us Jesus so that You could get us. Amen.

God Understands

Scripture Reading

"But he was pierced for our transgressions, he was crushed for our iniquities" (Isaiah 53:5).

Meditation

The cross reminds us that God is not blind to the way we live here on earth. He understands greed, unfaithfulness, dishonesty, hatred, and anger. He is not blind; He sees some of that in us. He sees us wrestling with those temptations, and at times yielding to them. He rebounded against our sins with His love. On the cross, those sins of ours, known clearly by God, have been drowned in the ocean of His grace and in the sea of His mercy.

Prayer

Thank You, Father, for coming down here on earth and living among us. You saw it from Heaven. You saw it on earth—what we are like. And in spite of that, You still love us and gave Your Son for us. Help us to grow in that love. Amen.

Take Up the Cross

Scripture Reading

"The punishment that brought us peace

was upon Him, and by his wounds we are healed" (Isaiah 53:5).

Meditation

Our sins separated us from God. They dislodged us from the unity we had with Him. They built a wall of alienation. Rebellion always expresses animosity—and that animosity describes sin. Rebellion shatters peace. But the story does not end there.

Peace came through punishment and healing came through wounds. Jesus did not find it easy. He found it painful. He found it shameful to be put on a cross. He found it lonely. Sometimes we will find punishment, pain, shame, and loneliness when we go to bat for others who need reconciliation and forgiveness. But Jesus meant just that when He said, "Take up Your cross and follow me."

Prayer

Bring to our minds, Father, any who hurt and need our healing touch; any who stand alone and need our friendly reach of peace—even when it's painful for us to do so. Amen.

It's for All

Scripture Reading

"We all, like sheep, have gone astray, each of us has turned to his own way; and the Lord has laid on him the iniquity of us all" (Isaiah 53:6).

Meditation

No one has escaped it. We have all fallen short of the character of God. When God reached down with forgiveness in the crucifixion of Jesus, He reached down to each of us—not a few of us, not many of us, but all of us. All of us have gone astray like sheep; but the Good Shepherd went looking—not for some, not for many, but for all—for you and me. God laid on Him the iniquity—not some of it, not a lot of it, but all of it.

Prayer

Sometimes it may seem like You love them but not "me." Let each of us know that You love "me," the "me" that picks up the bread and cup. It was for that "me" that Jesus died and rose and is coming again. Thank You, Father. Amen.

His Silence—Our Salvation

Scripture Reading

"He was oppressed and afflicted, yet he did not open his mouth; he was led like a lamb to the slaughter, and as a sheep before her shearers is silent, so he did not open his mouth" (Isaiah 53:7).

Meditation

Jesus could have stopped the crucifixion. He could have opened His mouth and said, "No, Father. I choose not to go to the cross." As the Lord of angels, He could have ordered thousands of them to come and wipe out His accusers. But He did neither. He opened not His mouth. His silence declared, "I love You." Now in our silence, let us declare in our hearts, "Lord, I love You."

Prayer

Father, sometimes when we are mad we stay silent in nonverbal retaliation. At other times we stay silent out of cowardice. But there are those times of deep emotion when our silence is a positive act of love. Take our silence now and hear our hearts beat our love to You. Amen.

Condemning Condemnation

Scripture Reading

"Yet it was the Lord's will to crush him and cause him to suffer, and though the Lord makes his life a guilt offering, he will see his offspring and prolong his days, and the will of the Lord will prosper in his hand" (Isaiah 53:10).

Meditation

Jesus did not go to the cross behind His Father's back. "It was the Lord's will to crush him and cause him to suffer." Jesus prayed in the Garden, "Let this cup pass from me." But the Father said "no" to Jesus in order to say "yes" to us. "No" to Jesus' escape from the cross and "yes" to our escape from condemnation. For in Christ there is no condemnation. What a love; what a grace; what a Father; what a God!

Prayer

In the midst of our rushed world, sometimes we forget just how much You are for us, Father. Thank You for not competing against us. Thank You for not manipulating us or trying to sell us something we don't need. Thank You for not comparing us with others. Thank You for giving Jesus no escape so that we could have escape through Him. Amen.

Guilt

Scripture Reading

"Yet it was the Lord's will to crush him and to cause him to suffer, and though the Lord makes his life a guilt offering, he will see his offspring and prolong his days and the will of the Lord will prosper in his hand" (Isaiah 53:10).

Meditation

On the cross our Lord did not just take away our sin as a whitewash job, but He also took away our guilt as a total soul wash. A courtroom judge today can declare a guilty person to be acquitted because of some technicality, but that doesn't really take away the guilt of the crime, nor will it erase the guilty feeling of the person. But God's power surpasses man's. He can declare us acquitted and enable us to be cleansed from guilt. Jesus became our guilt offering. If you still feel guilty, you feel wrong. He took our guilt; why try to take it back?

Prayer

Father, thank You for reminding us that when our hearts condemn us, You are greater than our hearts. When Jesus comes again, thank You that we will live with confidence in His presence. Thank You for taking care of the guilt in our souls. Amen.

He Stands for You

Scripture Reading

" . . . for he bore the sin of many, and

made intercession for the transgressors" (Isaiah 53:12).

Meditation

As an intercessor, Jesus became our stand-in. That means He stood in our place before the judge and took our sins as His. The Father accepted that. But that is not all. Right now Jesus sits at the right hand of the Father and continues to make intercession for us. He knows our troubles and needs. He knows our disappointments, our dreams, our doings, and our delights. He discusses them with the Father on our behalf. Someone prays for you, and we know Him as Jesus.

Prayer

Our Father, while we are thanking You for Jesus, we know that Jesus is talking to You and interceding for us. Keep us mindful, Father, that we never walk alone when we come to You. Amen.

Status That Counts

Scripture Reading

"Therefore I will give him a portion among the great, and he will divide the spoils with the strong, because he poured out his life unto death, and was numbered with the transgressors" (Isaiah 53:12).

Meditation

The benefits of Jesus' death did not end with the humiliation of the crucifixion. Because of His sacrificial love, God exalted Him to the highest place and gave Him a name above every name. Through the cross we learn that status comes through service. Exaltation comes through humility. A crown comes through the cross. Jesus said the greatest one among you will be the one who serves others. Then Jesus proved it by serving us as He hung on that cross.

Prayer

Help us not to seek so much to get as to give, not so much seek to be understood as to understand, not so much seek to hoard as to share, not so much seek to receive honor as to give honor, and not so much seek to protect self as to invest self for the betterment of others. Help us to see Jesus on the cross and to take up the cross ourselves as His followers. Amen.

He Doesn't Count

Scripture Reading

"God was reconciling the world to himself in Christ, not counting men's sins against them" (2 Corinthians 5:19).

Meditation

We live in a culture that likes to count. We count calories, memberships, money, Christmas cards received, and times we have been invited out. We count people, meetings, minutes, years, and pounds.

Isn't it great to know there is something that God does not count? He does not count our sins against us. For the forgiven person, the sins are never added up by God. Instead He erases them. Our sins are blotted out—eliminated—from any Heavenly record.

Prayer

Precious Savior, it seems too good to be true that nothing is counted against us. Thank You for leaving us the reminder in the bread and the cup. As we remember the sacrifice and the cancellation of our sins, we accept Your promise. Amen.

Newness

Scripture Reading

"Therefore, if anyone is in Christ, he is a new creation; the old has gone, the new has come!" (2 Corinthians 5:17).

Meditation

How are we a "new creation" when we become a Christian? We look the same, but we have a new beginning—we are born again; a new security—death and resurrection of Jesus; a new future—eternity in Heaven; a new family—the church; a new past—the old has gone; a new power—the Holy Spirit; a new nature—the Divine nature; a new growth—growing into Christlikeness; a new relationship—reconciled to God; and a new purpose—a servant and ambassador.

Prayer

There are times when we have thought about a second chance at life, God. We have thought, "What would it be like if we could go back and do it again?" But what we cannot do, You have done in Christ. You have given us a new start. We praise You for that gift. Amen.

Brokenness Mended

Scripture Reading

"God made him who had no sin to be sin for us, so that in him we might become the righteousness of God" (2 Corinthians 5:21).

Meditation

We have all fallen short of the glory of God. We have hurt and been hurt, broken and been broken, alienated and been alienated, wronged and been wronged, sinned and been sinned against.

But now as this time reminds us of God's grace, we bring to the Lord all the broken pieces of our lives and ask him to continue to put them together and make us whole. We give Him our ugliness, and He brings beauty out of it. We bring Him our weakness, and He makes us strong.

Prayer

It has been a great week for some people. Everything has fallen into place, so they find it is easy to commune with You, Father. But for others, things have fallen apart. They are in the pits and the valley. They may not find it easy. They must, however, meditate upon You. We are so thankful that You have invited us to Your table in spite of our failures. Amen.

The Camouflage Uncovered

Scripture Reading

"He himself bore our sins in his body on the tree, so that we might die to sin and live for righteousness; by his wounds you have been healed" (1 Peter 2:24).

Meditation

On the cross, we see truth fully exposed —truth about us, truth about pride, truth about selfishness, truth about unfaithfulness, truth about lust, truth about envy. The truth revealed itself at the foot of the cross. But it did not stay there. God placed it on the cross in Christ. We also see the truth about God, to whom Jesus said, "Father, forgive them." We sinned, but God loved. We took, but God gave. We rejected, but God accepted.

Prayer

We are such self-sufficient people, God. We like to do things ourselves. We cringe to think about how our sins were placed in His body on the tree. We like to overcome our own problems, but now we confess that no other way exists to be saved except in Jesus. Thank You. Amen.

The Great Return

Scripture Reading

"For you were like sheep going astray, but now you have returned to the Shepherd and Overseer of your souls" (1 Peter 2:25).

Meditation

This one sentence describes what happened when we became Christians. We returned to the Shepherd of our souls. This Shepherd leads us, heals the wounded, carries the weary, and strengthens the weak. He meets our needs, forces us to rest, stays with us through the storms, and conquers our enemies. Because of what Christ did on the cross, we know that the Good Shepherd is for us. Because of Him, we can say "surely goodness and love will follow me all the days of my life, and I will dwell in the house of the Lord forever."

Prayer

Thank You, Lord, for seeing that we wandered like sheep without a shepherd. Instead of blaming us, instead of calling us "stupid," instead of giving up on us, You came. You found us. Now You are our Shepherd and we shall not want. Amen.

The Emancipation

Scripture Reading

"When the hour came, Jesus and his apostles reclined at the table. And he said to them, 'I have eagerly desired to eat this Passover with you before I suffer'" (Luke 22:14, 15).

Meditation

Jesus instituted the Lord's Supper as He shared the Passover with His disciples. A connection exists between the Lord's Supper and the Passover. The Passover meal celebrated the Jews, leaving slavery under the Egyptian Pharaoh. The Lord's Supper celebrates Christians leaving slavery under the devil. The Passover reminded the Jews that they had made a break from the past with a new start for the future. The Lord's Supper reminds the Christians that we have been born again.

Prayer

It's amazing to us how much patience You had with the Israelites. You brought them out of Egypt, God, but they seemed so ungrateful and so so immature. They complained and rebelled. Through them, we see ourselves in a mirror. Thank You for loving us and exercising patience with us as well. Amen.

God's By-Pass Surgery

Scripture Reading

"The next day John saw Jesus coming toward him and said, 'Look the Lamb of God, who takes away the sin of the world!'" (John 1:29).

Meditation

Paul put it this way in 1 Corinthians 5:7, "For Christ, our Passover lamb, has been sacrificed." Death was coming to Egypt, but God had a plan for His people to by-pass it. The lamb was slaughtered, and blood was put on the top and sides of the door frame of individual houses. When the Lord saw that blood, death passed over those houses—thus the term "Passover Lamb." God has done it for us through His lamb—Jesus. Because Christ took our sins away, eternal death passes over us. We find our passover in Christ, and our Communion time celebrates Him.

Prayer

We are reminded what Your Son promised us, Father. "I tell you the truth, whoever hears my word and believes . . . has eternal life and will not be condemned." When we wonder if we can actually find truth in this, we are reminded that You proved it by raising Jesus from the dead. No one else could do that. Thank You. Amen.

How Often Is Too Much?

Scripture Reading

"This is my body, . . . do this in remembrance of me. . . . This cup is the new covenant in my blood; do this, whenever you drink it, in remembrance of me" (1 Corinthians 11:24, 25).

Meditation

Isn't once in a lifetime or once in a year or once in a month enough to say, "I love you"? Not really. Why do we leave pictures of people we love hanging on the wall or lying on the mantel? Wouldn't having them out occasionally be enough? Not really. When does the frequency of an event turn it into such familiarity that it becomes commonplace and thus no longer meaningful? Does eating two or three times a day do that? Does talking with a friend once a week do that? Does looking into the mirror in the morning do that? What becomes meaningful and meaningless is not tied to schedules but to our hearts. That's why Jesus said, "whenever" you do this, and Paul said, "as often as" you do this. The more we love someone, the more we want to commune with him.

Prayer

Forgive us, Father, for being excited about being with that special person we love and feeling empty when we are not with him—while at the same time, not anticipating—with You or not even missing it. Increase our love. Amen.

Our Memo Pad

Scripture Reading

"This is my body, . . . do this in remembrance of me. . . . This cup is the new covenant in my blood; do this, whenever you drink it, in remembrance of me" (1 Corinthians 11:24, 25).

Meditation

We know that we are forgetful people. That's why we write ourselves notes and send memos, keep appointment calendars, take pictures, keep scrapbooks, and keep a record of our checkbook balance. We use many ways to help us remember—making lists, looking into a mirror, or even asking others to remind us. Forgetful? Yes, we are, and God knows it. He instituted a way for us to remember what it took for us to be His children, to be brothers and sisters to one another, to be forgiven, and be able to worship in celebration. It took the sacrifice of His Son on the cross. That is why we should partake of God's holy meal—the Lord's Supper.

Prayer

Father, we thank You for remembering and forgetting. You forget our sins, but You remember us. Help us to remember what You remember and to forget what You forget. In the midst of the hustle and bustle of life, we confess it is easy for the importance of Jesus' death to slip from our minds. Remind us of His crucifixion each time we worship. Amen.

As a Servant

Scripture Reading

"Also a dispute arose among them as to which of them was considered to be the greatest. . . . For who is greater, the one who is at the table or the one who serves? Is it not the one who is at the table? But I am among you as one who serves" (Luke 22:24, 27).

Meditation

It happened around the table when Jesus had instituted the Lord's Supper. He had just declared that He was going to make the living sacrifice for them—and us. The disciples got into an argument among themselves as to which one of them was the greatest. Jesus replied to them that the greatest one is not the person who has the most servants serving him, but the person who voluntarily serves others. Jesus came as a server and elsewhere declared, "Whoever wants to be first must be your slave—just as the Son of Man did not come to be served, but to serve, and to give His life as a ransom for many."

Nowhere are we reminded of His service to us more clearly than during the Lord's Supper when we remember that His body was broken and His blood was shed as a ransom for us.

Prayer

Father, we remember that we have salvation because He served. We can live because He died. We are healed because He was wounded. Help us, as His disciples, to grow in service by thinking before speaking, by hearing before judging, by helping instead of hindering, by building up instead of tearing down others. Amen.

Something New

Scripture Reading

"I received from the Lord what I also passed on to you. The Lord Jesus on the night he was betrayed, took bread, and when he had given thanks, he broke it and said, 'This is my body, which is for you; do this in remembrance of me.' In the same way, after supper he took the cup, saying, 'This cup is the new covenant in my blood; do this, whenever you drink it, in remembrance of me'" (1 Corinthians 11:23, 24).

Meditation

How is this cup the new covenant in Jesus'

blood? What is new about it? Several things: first of all, sins are forgotten as well as forgiven—that's new. Second, earthly priests had to make a sacrifice for their own sins; Jesus was sinless and made a sacrifice only for others—that's new. Third, earthly priests came into the temple, a building; Jesus comes into the temple of our bodies—that's new. Fourth, the old covenant included the blood of goats and bulls. The new covenant included only the blood of Jesus—that's new. Fifth, sin sacrifices had to be made every year under the old covenant; Jesus made His sacrifice only once—that's new. Finally, under the old covenant, we would have had to bring the sacrifices; Jesus provided the sacrifice for us—himself—that's new.

Prayer

Father, help each of us to realize that although Jesus' death happened so long ago, the meaning is always refreshing and new for us today. Help us to be open to the renewal it brings.

Only Once for All

Scripture Reading

"Day after day every priest stands and performs his religious duties, again and again he offers the same sacrifices; which can never take away sins. But when this priest had offered for all time one sacrifice for sins, he sat down at the right hand of God" (Hebrews 10:11, 12).

Meditation

The sacrifices of the Old Testament never took away sins. They just stored up those sins until the great sacrifice was made for mankind. Jesus did not sacrifice many times only to a select few and not just for a year. He only sacrificed once for all people for all time. How marvelous! The sinless for the sinful; the perfect for the imperfect; the divine for the human; the Son of God for the sons of men. How effective! Only once, for all people, for all time.

Prayer

Our Father, at this time we remember the awesomeness of Your Son! We have to eat repeatedly because we hunger; we have to rest repeatedly because we tire; we have to exercise repeatedly because we deteriorate physically; but Jesus died—once, for all of us, for all time! A gift beyond comprehension—Thank You. Amen.

The Towel and the Tree

Scripture Reading

"After that, he poured water into a basin and began to wash his disciples' feet, drying them with the towel that was wrapped around him" (John 13:5).

Meditation

The place? The upper room. The situation? Institution of the Lord's Supper. The surprise? Jesus got up and washed twenty-four dirty feet. Wouldn't such a mundane activity break the spirit of the Lord's Supper? No—in fact, it helped communicate the significance of the Lord's Supper. The men were tired and had dirty feet. Jesus saw their need and moved to meet it. On that night in the few hours that followed, Jesus made it clear that no need was too small for Him, thus the towel. Also, no need was too big for Him—the sins of all mankind—thus the tree. This reminds us that He cares and acts.

Prayer

Help us to realize that Jesus did not go to the tree without picking up the towel. He did not die for men without living for them. As He died for us then, He continues to live for us now. Thank You for being consistent. Amen.

A Love Feast

Scripture Reading

"A new command I give you: Love one another. As I have loved you, so you must love one another. All men will know that you are my disciples if you love one another" (John 13:34, 35).

Meditation

Jesus had expressed His love during the Lord's Supper, and then He commanded His disciples to love as Jesus loved. We need to evaluate our love for God and Jesus as well as for one another. We need to measure our grace, our mercy, our forgiveness—for people will know we are His disciples by these attitudes. It is not how well we do with the bread, but how well we do with benevolence. It is not how well we do with the cup, but how well we do with compassion.

Prayer

Father, create in us a pure heart and renew a steadfast spirit within us so that Your kind of love can flow freely through us to the hatred, the hurt, and the disappointments of others. Amen.

Love on a Cross

Scripture Reading

"For God so loved the world that he gave his one and only Son, that whoever believes in him should not perish but have eternal life" (John 3:16).

Meditation

From the accusers' side, the cross symbolized injustice, jealousy, and hatred. From God's side, the cross symbolized love. On the cross we see love demonstrated. Love is patient. In the cross, God said, "I am willing to put up with you." Love is kind. In the cross, God said, "I am willing to overlook your past." Love is not proud. In the cross, God said, "I am willing to identify with you and your sins." Love is not self-seeking. On the cross, God said, "I am willing to give lavishly for your benefit." Love keeps no record of wrongs. On the cross, God said, "I forgive." Love does not delight in evil. On the cross, God said, "I want to put a stop to sin; I will nail it to the cross."

Prayer

Thank You, God, for allowing Jesus to become the Son of Man so that we, the sons of men, can become the sons of God. Thank You for Your love—that is shown, not only in Your words, but also in what You have done and continue to do for us.

Nearness from a Distance

Scripture Reading

"I in them and you in me. May they be brought to complete unity to let the world know that you sent me and have loved them even as you have loved me" (John 17:23).

Meditation

Between the time Jesus instituted the Lord's Supper and was arrested, He prayed this prayer. The cross was God's act to unite us. Paul wrote that we are reconciled—or united—through the cross. Before man sinned, he existed in complete unity with God, with himself, and with his fellowman. But when he sinned, in set disunity. He hid from God; he was ashamed of self; and he blamed his mate. In Christ we are God's child; that is, we have a relationship with God. In Christ we have forgiveness of sins; that is, we have a better relationship with self. In Christ we belong to one another; that is, we have a relationship with others. The blood of Christ brings those afar off nearer to God.

Prayer

Sometimes we slip back into the old nature. We resent You sometimes. We shame ourselves often. We cast the blame upon others. Help us to seek to deepen our love for You, for self, and for others. We thank You for Christ who makes this possible. Amen.

Accepting Denial

Scripture Reading

"Then he said to them all 'If anyone would come after me, he must deny himself and take up his cross daily and follow me'" (Luke 9:23).

Meditation

We know that we should fulfill our commitment of cross bearing, as God and Jesus fulfilled their commitment on the cross. Some see the cross as a place of hurting. Do we protect ourselves too much? When we bear the cross, we willingly accept rejection for that which is right. Do we seek acceptance by others and thus compromise our standards? When we bear the cross, we willingly go to bat for others who have made mistakes. Are we willing to reach out, to touch, and to befriend those who fall?

Prayer

Because of the cross and our acceptance of Jesus, You have placed Your divine nature in us. May that divine nature and power within our soul keep us bearing the cross now, just as Jesus did then. Amen.

The Open Door

Scripture Reading

"I am the gate; whoever enters through me will be saved. He will come in and go out, and find pasture" (John 10:9).

Meditation

What Jesus did on the cross provided the door or gateway for us. He is the door to the Father. Through that door we find forgiveness. We can also find the Holy Spirit when we walk through that door. He is our doorway to peace, to hope, to love, to resurrection, and to eternal life. Paul said, "Through him we both have access to the Father by one Spirit."

Prayer

Father, we live in such a fast-paced world that we feel so shut out from You, detached from ourselves, and isolated from others—even in the church. Help us to feel Your comfort and the promise of the abundant life come to pass. Help us to walk through the doorway to all that is worthwhile. Amen.

The Day Death Died

Scripture Reading

"But we see Jesus, who was made a little lower than the angels, now crowned with glory and honor because he suffered death, so that by the grace of God he might taste death for everyone" (Hebrews 2:9).

Meditation

In the ancient days, some slaves had the job of tasting a meal before it was served to the king in case the meal had been poisoned. Thus the slave would save the life of the king. Jesus did that for us. He "tasted death," not by merely sipping at it, but by fully draining the cup. To say, "for everyone" shows that He was God's universal substitution. The word "for" comes from a word that means "in the benefit of" or "for the sake of." And "everyone" includes us all. The day Jesus died was the day death died for those who are in Christ. We are celebrating that day.

Prayer

We thank You, Father, for allowing Your Son to taste the bitterness of death so that we might take in the blessings of life. Heal us when we allow that bitterness to hide the blessings. Amen.

Empty Power

Scripture Reading

"But they shouted, 'Take him away! Take him away! Crucify him!'

"'Shall I crucify your king?' Pilate asked.

"'We have no king but Caesar,' the chief priest answered. Finally Pilate handed him over to them to be crucified" (John 19:15, 16).

Meditation

The political and religious powers of the time teamed up to crucify Jesus. But when Jesus resurrected, He exposed the emptiness of mere worldly power. He knew that God's power surpasses man's. He faced misguided accusations with grace and dignity. Do we try to live our lives with power plays today? The cross and resurrection prove that God's will outperforms the games men play.

Prayer

You have enabled us to have access to Your Spirit. Help us to be filled with Your Spirit—that Spirit of love, joy, peace, and patience—and to be emptied of our own selfish spirits, so that the triumphant power of Christ can shine through us. Amen.

Death That Speaks

Scripture Reading

"Now the Feast of Unleavened Bread, called the Passover, was approaching, and the chief priests and the teachers of the law were looking for some way to get rid of Jesus" (Luke 22:1, 2).

Meditation

Jesus understood that His preaching and teaching offended the established powers of His day. He had ample opportunity to change His teachings and to compromise, as well as to stay away from the center of the opposition in Jerusalem. But He believed that His message had to be taken to the very center of Judean life. He could have assured the Jewish and Roman leaders that His teachings would no longer challenge their life-styles, but He knew that God's message had to be taken to the very place where man's thoughts were being formed. He died so that God's message would live on forever through His followers.

Prayer

Lord, help us remember Jesus' courage—and then to match ours to His. Amen.

God Is With Us

Scripture Reading

"The virgin will be with child and will give birth to a son, and they will call him 'Immanuel'—which means 'God with us'" (Matthew 1:23).

Meditation

Notice that He is not just God over us, although He is. He is not just God above us, although He is. He is not just God under us to support us, although He is. But He is God *with* us. He came to bridge the gap between us and God. He came to be with us because He likes us. More than that, He loves us. He died so that we could be with Him forever.

Prayer

Sometimes we feel like no one knows us, likes us, or wants us. Thank You for coming to brush shoulders with us and for wanting us to be with You throughout all eternity. Amen.

20/20 Vision

Scripture Reading

"Therefore let all Israel be assured of this: God has made this Jesus, whom you crucified, both Lord and Christ" (Acts 2:36).

Meditation

When orthodox Jews read the Old Testament and came to the word "God," they substituted the word "Lord," because the word "God" was so sacred to them. The word "Christ" meant *anointed one* and was used by the Jews to refer to their special messengers anointed by God to be His stand-ins. When Peter said that Jesus was both Lord and Christ, they understood that God had visited them in the form of Jesus, and the anointed Savior for whom they had been looking had come. But they had abused Him. As soon as Peter made that declaration, the people were cut to the heart, and said, "Brothers, what shall we do?"

Three thousand repented and were baptized that day. Thus began the church. The people on Pentecost saw Jesus correctly. May we continue today to communicate Christ correctly.

Prayer

Father, cut us to the heart again as we meditate upon a man who walked on this earth with kindness, gentleness, patience, grace, and sacrifice. You Yourself made this man. May we never take You for granted or abuse You. Lead us into repentance this day. Amen.

Part 2: Offering Meditations

God First

Scripture Reading

"Honor the Lord with your wealth, and the first fruits of all your crops" (Proverbs 3:9).

Meditation

Honoring God and offering the first fruits relate to each other. A farmer does not honor God by waiting to see if he has any crops left over for God. He honors God by giving Him the first portion. Isn't that what God did for us? He gave us His first portion when He gave us His Son. He gave us His *only* portion—His only begotten son. When we get our paycheck and immediately think, "I am setting aside a certain amount for God before any other expenses"—that is real honor.

Prayer

We thank You, Father, for not putting us off till last, but thinking of us first. We worship You for not giving us Your leftovers. You gave us Your first and finest. We have riches throughout eternity because of that gift. Amen.

Our "Real" Estate

Scripture Reading

"Whoever can be trusted with very little can also be trusted with much, and whoever is dishonest with very little will also be dishonest with much. So if you have not been trustworthy in handling worldly wealth, who will trust you with true riches? And if you have not been trustworthy with someone else's property, who will give you property of your own?" (Luke 16:10-12).

Meditation

We find worldly wealth in this life. We find true riches after death. The text mentions "someone else's property." That's God's property that we use in this life. God will give us property of our own in eternity and for eternity. That's our "real" estate property. We can find a relationship between our rewards then and our generosity now.

Prayer

Help us to realize Your ownership of us and teach us to give to others what You have given us, dear God. Amen.

No U-Haul There

Scripture Reading

"Do not store up for yourselves treasures on earth, where moth and rust destroy, and where thieves break in and steal. But store up for yourselves treasures in heaven, where moth and rust do not destroy, and where thieves do not break in and steal" (Matthew 6:19, 20).

Meditation

Jesus has nothing against savings accounts, but He teaches against prioritizing the temporary—that which is on earth—instead of prioritizing the permanent—that which is in Heaven. All we have here exists temporarily; others will have it when we die. Ever seen a hearse pull a U-Haul to the cemetery? While we will take no treasures to the cemetery with us, we will take treasures to Heaven with us through our generosity.

Prayer

Remind us, God, of how we have only temporary things. Teach us to lessen our grip on these passing things and tighten our hold on the permanent treasures. Amen.

A Love Gift

Scripture Reading

"For God so loved the world that he gave his one and only Son, that whoever believes in him shall not perish but have eternal life" (John 3:16).

Meditation

A direct relationship exists between loving and giving. Giving expresses love. Hoarding does not. Can you imagine saying to your children or to your mate, "I love you, but I am not using any of my worldly wealth for you"? How can we, then, say that to God? During this time we express our love to God in an objective and sacrificial way. On the cross God declares, "This is my love for you." He made a love-gift. For giving expresses loving, and loving expresses giving.

Prayer

O God, the source of love, we admit to You that You love us and we know it. We know it because of the actions and effort expended for us. May You know now in this moment as we give that we love You. Amen.

Attitudes and Altitude

Scripture Reading

"The wicked borrow and do not repay, but the righteous give generously" (Psalm 37:21).

Meditation

We can possibly develop several attitudes about wealth. First, "What is yours is mine and I will take it." This attitude will lead to stealing. Second, "What is mine is mine and I will spend it." This attitude may lead to reckless extravagance. Third, "What is mine is mine and I will hoard it." This attitude may lead to worry and isolationism. Fourth, "What is mine is God's and I will always use part of it for His desires—all of it, should He ask for it." This attitude will lead to generosity, fulfillment, peace, and meaningfulness in living. Only the latter demonstrates a Godlike mindset. Our attitude determines our altitude.

Prayer

Thank You, Father, for sharing with us of Your abundance. Thank You that You give rather than take. In Your patience with us, gently lead us to become more like You in Your generosity. Amen.

Newness and Old Money

Scripture Reading

"You were taught, with regard to your former way of life, to put off your old self, which is being corrupted by its deceitful desires; to be made new in the attitude of your minds; and to put on the new self, created to be like God in true righteousness and holiness" (Ephesians 4:22-24).

Meditation

Becoming a Christian means putting on the new self created to be like God. To do this means to be born again. Then the Christian grows into Godlikeness. God demonstrates His character by giving. He gives love and forgiveness. He gives His Son and His Spirit. Best of all He will give us Heaven. We grow into His likeness as we give away that which we deem valuable. Old money takes on new meaning when we consider our birth and our new family.

Prayer

Father, we are all children in different stages of growth. We confess to You that we like having things, and we thank You for that opportunity. We confess that we know what it means to say "mine." Teach us,

Lord, the joy of saying "not mine but thine" as did our Lord Jesus. Amen.

Wealth and Friends

Scripture Reading

"I tell you, use worldly wealth to gain friends for yourselves, so that when it is gone, you will be welcomed into eternal dwellings" (Luke 16:9).

Meditation

Jesus spoke these words. He wants us to use our worldly wealth in ways that will help others to get to Heaven—and thus gain eternal friends. When our wealth goes—and all of it will be gone when we die, if not before—some of those people who have become Christians through our resources and who get to Heaven before us will be there to greet us. How regularly and how sacrificially are we making friends for ourselves in Heaven by our giving?

Prayer

Father, we mourn to have our loved ones go before us in death, but we rejoice to know that they will welcome us into eternal dwellings. Thank You, Father, for letting us know that people whom we have not yet met but who have become Christians, partly through our giving, have become our friends in Christ and will welcome us. Amen.

A Healthy Body

Scripture Reading

"Now you are the body of Christ, and each one of you is a part of it" (1 Corinthians 12:27).

"From him the whole body, joined and held together by every supporting ligament, grows and builds itself up in love, as each part does its work" (Ephesians 4:16).

Meditation

A national survey shows that only twenty percent of church members give any of their wealth for the life, mission, and activities of the church. How that must sadden Christ. The church is the body of Christ. Just as in our physical bodies, individual parts become healthier as they contribute. The health of Christ's body depends upon the way individual parts share with each other and for each other. Help give our Head, Jesus, a healthy body. He deserves it.

Prayer

Father, how we yearn for every part of our physical body to share its benefits with the other parts. As a part of Christ's body, help us to function in our privilege of giving and thus benefit the whole body. Amen.

Our Mortgage and Our Master

Scripture Reading

"There is no need for me to write to you about this service to the saints. For I know your eagerness to help, and I have been boasting about it to the Macedonians, telling them that since last year you in Achaia were ready to give; and your enthusiasm has stirred most of them to action" (2 Corinthians 9:1, 2).

Meditation

The Corinthians made a commitment to give. Paul encouraged them to carry it out. Have you ever heard anyone say, "I don't believe in making a commitment to the church or the Lord's work"? We make many commitments in life. We commit to a telephone company, to an electric company, to a trash pick-up company, to the water department, to a mortgage company, and others. Remember how eager we were to commit to a mortgage and what a sense of fulfillment it was to move into that house? God is better than all of that. Can we be as eager to commit to give to the Master?

Prayer

Thank You, Father, for making promises to us and keeping them. We know that You are faithful to carry out every promise. Accept our gifts today as an expression of our worship and thankfulness through Christ. Amen.

Our Voting Record

Scripture Reading

"But if serving the Lord seems undesirable to you, then choose for yourselves this day whom you will serve, whether the gods your forefathers served beyond the River, or the gods of the Amorites, in whose land you are living. But as for me and my household, we will serve the Lord" (Joshua 24:15).

Meditation

Nearly every year the government holds an election—either an election in the city, the state, or the nation. Our giving represents a voting record for us. In our giving, we vote that we want God's values, priorities, principles, life-style, Word, compassion, grace, forgiveness, and salvation to continue. We don't want to vote Him out. What voting record do you have concerning your giving? We write the record today.

Prayer

Father, remain with us this week and keep us diligent in our work, humble in our estimation of ourselves, kind in our dealings with others, mindful of our kinship with You, and now generous with the things we have. Amen.

Diluted Juice

Scripture Reading

"Yet it was good of you to share in my troubles. Moreover, as you Philippians know, in the early days of your acquaintance with the gospel, when I set out from Macedonia, not one church shared with me in the matter of giving and receiving, except you only" (Philippians 4:14, 15).

Meditation

A village had a celebration and asked the people to bring a container of fresh juice for the festival. Crops were poor and juice was scarce and expensive. One person thought that since everyone else would bring juice, he would bring water—no one would know the difference. To the surprise of many at the festival, when the toast of juice for the president of the country who attended was given—the only drink was water. Everyone had thought the same and had brought water. Your gift united with gifts of everyone else makes all the difference for the continuation of Heaven's work on earth.

Prayer

To Your care, Father, we commend our family and our friends asking You to keep them safe in soul and body. We also commend to Your care those with whom we work and those sitting around us just now—and into Your care, we commend our gifts to blend in with the gifts of others to make a difference in the lives of people. Amen.

Be a Seeker

Scripture Reading

"But seek first his kingdom and his righteousness, and all these things will be given to you as well" (Matthew 6:33).

Meditation

The Lord's Prayer provides an interesting example to follow. In it are these words, "Your kingdom come, Your will be done on earth as it is in heaven." Then comes the request, "Give us today our daily bread." Children of God will ask for daily bread—daily needs—so that we can have something to contribute to God's kingdom. In that way, we will be helping God's will to be done on earth. What a way to pray; what a way to live; what a reason to give. What a value to seek! Our giving expresses our seeking.

Prayer

Our Father which art in heaven, Hallowed by thy name. Thy kingdom come. Thy will be done; on earth, as it is in heaven. Give us this day our daily bread. And forgive us our debts as we forgive our debtors. Lead us not into temptation, but deliver us from evil: For thine is the kingdom, and the power, and the glory, for ever. Amen.

Engraved Palms

Scripture Reading

"This is how God showed his love among us: he sent his one and only Son into the world that we might live through him. This is love: not that we loved God, but that he loved us and sent his Son as an atoning sacrifice for our sins" (1 John 4:9, 10).

Meditation

We turn to the Lord and ask, "How much do You love me?" He stretches out His hands, points to the nail prints, and says, "This much." But as we look more closely into those hands, we see the truth of Isaiah 49:16, "I have engraved you on the palms of my hands." From the scars on His hands, we know His love for us—by name. Then He turns to us and asks, "How much do you love me?" He picks up our check-book, and asks, "This much?" Do we keep Him inscribed on that book?

Prayer

Father, we try Your patience, but You continue to drown our transgressions in the sea of Your eternal love. We confess to You, Father, it is so easy to be blind to the sufferings of others and so quick to harden our hearts to the needs of Your kingdom. Forgive and transform us. Amen.

When Little Becomes Much

Scripture Reading

"Jesus replied, 'They do not need to go away. You give them something to eat.'

"'We have here only five loaves of bread and two fish,' they answered" (Matthew 14:16, 17).

Meditation

They had only five loaves and two fish to nourish five thousand men plus women and children. Some disciples thought they had too little to make any difference in the need. We feel like that as we look at the spiritual needs of the world on the one hand and our resources on the other. Those disciples brought what they could find and put it in Jesus' hands. Jesus made little become much. Here we find this lesson: give it to Jesus, and He will do far more with it than we can when we keep it in our own hands.

Prayer

Father, continue to show us our smallness and Your greatness, our sin and Your purity, our lovelessness and Your love, our impotency and Your power. You can do far more than we ask or think. With the resources we give to You, do it again. Amen.

The "Foolish" Wisdom

Scripture Reading

"Then he said, 'This is what I will do. I will tear down my barns and build bigger ones, and there I will store all my grain and my goods. And I'll say to myself, "You have plenty of goods laid up for many years. Take life easy; eat, drink and be merry."'

"But God said to him, 'You fool! This very night your life will be demanded from you. Then who will get what you have prepared for yourself?'

"This is how it will be with anyone who stores up things for himself but is not rich toward God" (Luke 12:18-20).

Meditation

In just fifty-one words, that man referred to himself nine times. Every fifth word, he mentioned himself. Why did God call him a fool when elsewhere the Bible refers to the fool as one who does not believe that there is a God? This man's attitude showed that he was his own god. He used his property as his throne. To believe in God leads to belief in sharing, not hoarding. He showed wisdom in becoming rich, but foolishness in becoming selfish.

Prayer

We have things stored up for ourselves, but forgive us when we are rich toward ourselves and poor toward You. As You have saved us, now use us. Amen.

Misplaced Affections

Scripture Reading

"For the love of money is a root of all kinds of evil. Some people, eager for money, have wandered from the faith and pierced themselves with many griefs" (1 Timothy 6:10).

Meditation

Notice that the Scripture says that the money itself is not evil, but an affection for it. This affection can lead us to greed, jealousy, and cheating. It is the affection for money that can prevent us from contributing toward God's kingdom. As first priority, God places our affection, not our money. Only when we direct our affection toward Him can we master what we have instead of its mastering us.

Prayer

Only Your grace and generosity have anything at all to offer us. You write Your grace on our houses, on our bank accounts, on our cars, and across our clothes. May others see Your grace through our sharing. Amen.

God's Creative Plan

Scripture Reading

"So God created man in his own image, in the image of God he created him; male and female he created them" (Genesis 1:27).

Meditation

God is love and is the author of love. He created us to love Him, to love others, and to dominate over things. The source of problems in the world today can be found in how we have changed God's creative plan. Instead of loving God, loving one another and dominating over things, we fall in love with things and try to dominate one another and God. Sharing our wealth regularly for the benefit of others means returning to God's plan with our provisions.

Prayer

Lord, we collect things and discard people too easily. We pursue things and persecute people. We pursue happiness by getting rather than by giving. Make our thoughts Your thoughts and our ways Your ways. Breathe Your Spirit into us afresh and form our minds and incline our hearts to be like Yours. Amen.

The Heart That Follows

Scripture Reading

"For where your treasure is, there your heart will be also" (Matthew 6:21).

Meditation

Notice how that works. Buy a car and you will notice every car like it on the road. Buy some stocks and you will be interested in the reports from Wall Street. Our hearts will follow our treasure. God finds nothing wrong with having a car or stocks, but He wants our hearts to be on things eternal and non-destructible. We need to invest part of our treasure in Kingdom work. Our interest, our concerns, and our conduct will follow our investments.

Prayer

Father, You have invested in us and You have shown concern for us. Help us to make the right investments for the furtherance of Your kingdom—not within our selfishness. Thank You for the inheritance You have waiting for us in heaven. Amen.

A Command of Love

Scripture Reading

"Command them to do good, to be rich in good deeds, and to be generous and willing to share" (1 Timothy 6:18).

Meditation

We must consider generosity as a command, not an option. God is not interested in raising money, but raising up children to mature adults. Sometimes children do not share their toys. Their parents should teach them how to share. They should teach this not because they are interested in toys, but because they are interested in the maturity of their children. Parents know that toys are temporary, but their kids are permanent. They want them to grow up caring about others and sharing their things. By commanding us to share, God helps us have life and have it abundantly.

Prayer

Father, the older we get, the more childish we become. We confess that we like the words "me" and "mine." We like to grab the things we have and hold them close. Father, continue to teach us and command us to grow up into generous adults in Your family. Amen.

Jesus in Need

Scripture Reading

"Then the King will say to those on his right, 'Come, you who are blessed by my Father; take your inheritance, the kingdom prepared for you since the creation of the world. For I was hungry and you gave me something to eat, I was thirsty and you gave me something to drink, I was a stranger and you invited me in, I needed clothes and you clothed me, I was sick and you looked after me, I was in prison and you came to visit me'" (Matthew 25:34-36).

Meditation

When did we see Jesus have these needs and meet those needs by our personal involvement and sharing? Has anyone here ever seen Jesus in need? Jesus said, "Whatever you did for one of the least of these brothers of mine, you did for me." Not only do we minister to another person or situation through our giving, but we also minister directly to Jesus. He notices our giving and will remind us of it when He comes again. Our giving is *with* money, *through* people, and *to* Jesus.

Prayer

Father, we remember Jesus at this moment—His eagerness not to be ministered unto but to minister, His sympathy with the suffering, His sensitivity to share, and His words to us, "Follow me." Help us to do so. Amen.

God as Debtor

Scripture Reading

"He who is kind to the poor lends to the Lord, and he will reward him for what he has done" (Proverbs 19:17).

Meditation

Have you ever heard it said that God is no man's debtor? That is not true. God tells us that we make a loan to Him when we help the needy through our giving. That's because God has a big heart for the needy. God will repay us richly when Jesus comes again. Jesus promises that in sacrificing we will receive a hundred times as much and will also inherit eternal life. That's ten thousand per cent interest. No one shows more gratitude for our giving than God himself.

Prayer

Right now in our giving, You watch us, Father. This makes us uncomfortable. Couldn't You turn Your head this time? Better yet, help us to turn our hearts and face toward You as much in our giving as we do in our receiving. Amen.

Rich in Every Way

Scripture Reading

"You will be made rich in every way so that you can be generous on every occasion, and through us your generosity will result in thanksgiving to God" (2 Corinthians 9:11).

Meditation

To be made rich in every way does not necessarily mean we will have more money in the bank immediately after giving. It can mean that God will make us rich in attitudes, in generosity, in cheerfulness, in satisfaction, in contentment, in meaningfulness, in spiritual growth, in mental health, and in people sensitivity. No bank closing or stock market falling can delete those riches. We grow as we give.

Prayer

Let me today, O God, live as a Christian not only in how I received Your gifts in the past but how I give my gifts in the present, not only in how I have been served by You but in how I serve others, not only in how I have brought my needs to You in prayer but in how I bring Your resources to others. Help us to be truly Christian—walking in the footsteps of Jesus. Amen.

Planting Seed

Scripture Reading

"Now he who supplies seed to the sower and bread for food will also supply and increase your store of seed and will enlarge the harvest of your righteousness" (2 Corinthians 9:10).

Meditation

Use it and you won't lose it. It's like planting seed. More seed is supplied to the farmer when he puts it into the ground, for the seed produces more seed. God does for the Christian what He does for the farmer. For those who offer generosity and cheerfulness He promises to increase our store of seed and enlarge the harvest of our righteousness. The harvest here relates to the use of what God supplies. He supplies it so we can share it and reap an enlarging harvest of doing good.

Prayer

Our Father, guard us from giving with the only motivation to receive more from You. We want to be Jesus' followers and want to give as He gave. Amen.

From Giving to Thanksgiving

Scripture Reading

"This service that you perform is not only supplying the needs of God's people but is also overflowing in many expressions of thanks to God" (2 Corinthians 9:12).

Meditation

So much in this world gives God heartache and disappointment. Wouldn't you like to motivate more people to give to God? Wouldn't it be great if today and in the days that follow more people would look to God and say thank you? That happens through our giving. God promises people who receive the benefits of our giving will overflow in expressing thanks to God and in praising Him. Our giving directly affects God through the reaction of others. They may not know us, but they will affirm God; they will thank God because of *our* giving.

Prayer

O Father, we invite Christ to fill us in this moment with power for our weakness, courage for our fear, cleansing for our wrong, love for our hatred, joy for our sadness, and generosity for our stinginess. Amen.

Partnership

Scripture Reading

"And in their prayers for you their hearts will go out to you, because of the surpassing grace God has given you" (2 Corinthians 9:14).

Meditation

How many people pray for you? How many people would you like to pray for you? If you give, more people will pray for you than you have ever imagined. For Paul tells us that the recipients of our gifts—even though we may not meet or see many of them—will offer up prayers for us. The more we give, the more people are helped and the more prayers are lifted up to God for us. How wonderful! We act to meet needs, and the needy react with their prayers of thanksgiving. What a dividend!

Prayer

O Father, we cannot to see the immeasurable, unlimited, unrestrained possibilities in this gift of ours. Help us to give just because we respect You and care about Your wishes and leave the benefits in Your hands. Amen.

Giving Is Judging

Scripture Reading

"Give, and it will be given to you. A good measure, pressed down, shaken together and running over, will be poured into your lap. For with the measure you use, it will be measured to you" (Luke 6:38).

Meditation

We judge by our giving. For when we give, we judge that we should follow what God's Word says about giving. We judge that people who receive the benefits of our gifts deserve the worthiness of God's Son. If we refuse to give, we judge others to be worthy of condemnation.

Prayer

Father, thank You for measuring our worth and the worth of all others by the gift of Your Son. You bought us with Your precious love. Help us to not withhold what we know we cannot keep beyond the grave. Amen.

Risk-Taking

Scripture Reading

"Remember this: Whoever sows sparingly will also reap sparingly, and whoever sows generously will also reap generously" (2 Corinthians 9:6).

Meditation

Why give away what we can put away for interest? But God says what you give generously you will reap generously. That's not taking a risk. "You will abound in every good work" . . . that's not taking a risk. "He will supply and increase your store" . . . that's not taking a risk. "You will be made rich in every way so you can be generous on every occasion". . . that's not taking a risk. "God will meet all your needs according to His glorious riches in Christ Jesus" . . . that's not taking a risk. What is risky is not trusting God with our things, property, and wealth.

Prayer

O Father, thank You for taking the risk out of sharing our wealth. You never quit accepting, loving, and forgiving us. You are always reaching out to us. How awesome and faithful You are! Help us to increase our faithfulness to You. Amen.

The Good News

Scripture Reading

"Each man should give what he has decided in his heart to give, not reluctantly or under compulsion, for God loves a cheerful giver" (2 Corinthians 9:7).

Meditation

One of every ten verses in the Gospels—Matthew, Mark, Luke, and John—deals directly with money—288 verses in all. Is it because God is poor? No, no one is richer than God. Is it because God is interested in things? No, He is interested in us. He wants us to become more like Him. And He gives cheerfully. He loves to share. He wants us to enjoy the life that is life indeed—generosity will always bring cheerfulness. That's good news!

Prayer

Father, we stay so busy looking for ways to entertain ourselves—to laugh, to relax, to take a break, to be refreshed—and we confess that in our work at being happy, we often forget that happiness results from unselfishness. Help us to remember that. Amen.

The Abundant Smallness

Scripture Reading

"As he looked up, Jesus saw the rich putting their gifts into the temple treasury. He also saw a poor widow put in two very small copper coins. 'I tell you the truth,' he said, 'this poor widow has put in more than all the others. All these people gave their gifts out of their wealth; but she out of her poverty put in all she had to live on'" (Luke 21:1-4).

Meditation

God values our sharing more by our attitude than by the amount of the gift. The rich gave out of their surplus; the widow gave out of her shortage. They gave out of their comfort zone; she gave out of her discomfort. They gave out of reasoned calculation; she gave out of reasonable faith. They gave what they knew they could afford; she gave what she knew she could not afford. They gave what they did not need; she gave what she did need. Although the amount was small, Jesus said, she had put in more than all the others.

Prayer

O Father, You have touched us and given us treasures. You have given us all things that pertain to life and godliness. You have mapped out an eternity of riches for us. You are generous beyond calculation. We thank You. Amen.

What If?

Scripture Reading

"Let us not become weary in doing good, for at the proper time, we will reap a harvest if we do not give up. Therefore as we have opportunity, let us do good to all people, especially to those who belong to the family of believers" (Galatians 6:9, 10).

Meditation

What if Zaccheus waited until the next time to tell Jesus he was going to share his wealth? What if Mary who broke the bottle of perfume on Jesus' feet had waited—"I'll save it for a few events coming up first"—to give it to Jesus? What if the widow with the two small coins decided to wait until she had more to give? If they had delayed, they would have missed their golden moment. They would have missed the joy from giving generously and cheerfully.

Prayer

We have struggled with the what-if's. Thank You, God, for being patient with us. Fill us with Your Spirit of generosity and help us to give extravagantly with our provisions for the benefit of Your Kingdom. Amen.

A Plan That Works

Scripture Reading

"On the first day of every week, each one of you should set aside a sum of money in keeping with his income, saving it up, so that when I come no collections will have to be made" (1 Corinthians 16:2).

Meditation

There are several aspects of stewardship highlighted here: first, regular giving—we should give on the first day of every week; second, personal giving—God wants each one of us members to feel that responsibility; third, planned giving—we should set aside a sum of money, not as an afterthought but as a planned sacrifice; fourth, proportionate giving—each person should keep within his income and give, not with equal giving, but with equal sacrifice. Let us not forget to include our offerings as an essential part of our budget.

Prayer

Thank You, Father, for sending us away from the sidelines to participate with You in Your programs locally and around the world. You continually transform us from being people filled with greed to being people filled with Your grace. You remind us to cease from storing up for ourselves and remind us to share with others. Help us to seek involvement instead of isolation, fulfillment instead of meaninglessness. Amen.

God's Funnel

Scripture Reading

"All the believers were together and had everything in common. Selling their possessions and goods, they gave to anyone as he had need" (Acts 2:44, 45).

Meditation

Luke wrote these words just three verses after he reported the beginning of the church. People began the church by receiving the generosity of God's gift—the gift of forgiveness, of salvation, and of the Holy

Spirit. These people, the recipients of these gifts, continued the church by becoming givers. The Spirit of the generous God turned them into generous people. The church acts as God's funnel—grace in, grace out.

Prayer

Help me this day, Father, not to walk by anyone in need without caring. Help me to hear about those people who hurt. Keep us from closing off any corner of our lives from Your influence and continue to change us into the kind of people we know we can become. Amen.

Resurrection Giving

Scripture Reading

"And with great power the apostles were giving witness to the resurrection of the Lord Jesus, and abundant grace was upon them all" (Acts 4:33, *New American Standard Bible*).

Meditation

How in this context did they give witness to the resurrection of Jesus? The next verses tell us, "For there was not a needy person among them, for all who were owners of lands or houses would sell them and bring the proceeds of the sales, and lay them at the apostles' feet; and they would be distributed to each, as any had need." How does sharing testify to the resurrection of Christ? It demonstrates that Jesus is the Lord of all things—even our material things. Unselfishness in sharing shows that we believe that we will have a resurrection and God will enrich us. It shows that we believe people, not things, are eternal. Sharing shows that we believe not only that He lives today, but that He lives in us and that His generosity makes a difference.

Prayer

We thank You, Father, not only for giving us a livelihood, but also for giving us a new life. We thank You for material security that we have in our jobs, but more than that for Your Spirit that we receive through Jesus' resurrection. Thank You for making a difference in us because He lives. Amen.

Grabbers or Givers

Scripture Reading

"Command those who are rich in this present world not to be arrogant nor to put their hope in wealth, which is so uncertain, but to put their hope in God, who richly provides us with everything for our enjoyment" (1 Timothy 6:17).

Meditation

Did you notice it? God wants you to enjoy life. It is not wrong to use our provisions in ways that fill our hearts with joy. Why, after saying that, did Paul command that we be generous in sharing (v. 18)? He did it because sharing increases our joy. The hoarder finds only incompleteness with his treasures. Just ask Howard Hughes. The generous find enjoyment in giving. Just ask Mother Theresa.

Prayer

Now we can see, Father, why You have so much joy. You find joy in giving. We see that You have shared Your riches with us so that we can experience the joy that comes through generosity. Thank You for lifting us up to Your level of living. Amen.

Boomerang Giving

Scripture Reading

"In everything I did, I showed you that by this kind of hard work we must help the weak, remembering the words the Lord Jesus himself said, 'It is more blessed to give than to receive'" (Acts 20:35).

Meditation

Remember how hilariously happy we were as kids when we saw the gifts under the tree on Christmas morning? But most of us have gone through the transformation into adulthood of being more hilariously happy when we see our children and grandchildren open the gifts that we have given them. It is more blessed to give than to receive. In fact, it is a double blessing. The person to whom we give is blessed, and like a boomerang it comes back to bless us. Our benevolence comes back to us as His blessing.

Prayer

Thank You, God, for Your grace to us. Increase that grace—the grace of a thankful and uncomplaining heart; the grace of boldness, of standing for what is right; the grace to treat others as I would have others treat me; the grace of silence that I may refrain from hasty speech; the grace of tenderness toward all who are weaker than myself; and the grace of generosity for expanding Your Kingdom. Amen.

Robbing God

Scripture Reading

"He who has been stealing must steal no longer, but must work, doing something useful with his own hands, that he may have something to share with those in need" (Ephesians 4:28).

Meditation

Have you ever stolen? Are you stealing now? How were the Christians in Ephesus stealing? The Bible tells us that the earth is the Lord's and everything in it. All that we have God has delegated to us. The Bible calls us stewards—which means managers. God allows us to own for several reasons—enjoyment, providing for our families, and providing for the needs of others. If those three are not a regular part of our lives, we have misused God's property; that's one form of stealing. God said, "Yet you rob me." How? He said, "In tithes and offerings." God said it; He never lies.

Prayer

Almighty and Generous Father, we think of people who need Your help—those who face great temptation, those who face the valley of the shadow of death, those who overextend themselves in debt, those who wrestle with huge decisions, those who detach themselves from You and cannot hear Your good news. Channel us as messengers of Your help. Amen.

The Warning

Scripture Reading

"He answered, 'Then I beg you, father, send Lazarus to my father's house, for I have five brothers. Let him warn them, so that they will not also come to this place of torment'" (Luke 16:27, 28).

Meditation

After refusing to help the beggar Lazarus, a self-centered rich man spoke those words. The rich man got richer and the poor man got poorer. Then both the rich man and the beggar died. The rich cried in torment. About what did he want to warn his brothers? That God exists? No, the Jews believed that. That God created this world? No, the Jews believed that. Because the brothers inherited part of that man's wealth, he wanted them to be warned so they would be generous and make permanent investments for eternity with their temporary inheritance. The answer to that request was that they had been warned through God's prophets who spoke a great deal about helping the needy.

Prayer

Father, You clearly define generosity. You have been so simple in how You have told us to be generous people. We can't miss it; now, help us to mirror it—to mirror Christ. Amen.

Begging to Give

Scripture Reading

"For I testify that they gave as much as they were able, and even beyond their ability. Entirely on their own, they urgently pleaded with us for the privilege of sharing in this service to the saints" (2 Corinthians 8:3, 4).

Meditation

We have all seen beggars on the streets, and most of us have been approached by one. Beggars beg to receive; but have you ever met a person begging to give? Paul described some people who lived in extreme poverty, but they begged for the privilege of participating in the offering. They endured severe trials but had overflowing joy. They gave as much as they were able—even beyond their ability. They should have received; instead, they begged for the privilege of sharing. Notice that the positives override all of the negatives in their situation, because they saw sharing as a privilege—a way of participating with God.

Prayer

Father, we thank You for the privilege of

sharing. We relish the privilege to be partners with You and the privilege to please You. We beg to help others and to help expand Your Kingdom. Christ has made it possible. Amen.

Scoffers or Sharers

Scripture Reading

"The Pharisees, who loved money, heard all this and were sneering at Jesus" (Luke 16:14).

Meditation

What did those Pharisees hear? They heard Jesus say, "No servant can serve two masters. Either he will hate the one and love the other, or he will be devoted to the one and despise the other. You cannot serve both God and Money." Upon hearing that, they became scoffers, complainers, trouble-makers. How do we react when we hear talk about money in the church? Who or what is the object of our affection? Whom or what do we serve? Who or what gives us self-esteem and status? We must choose to be like either the complaining scoffers—the Pharisees—or a compassionate sharer—Jesus. It's our choice.

Prayer

Everyone around us wants some of our

money for their benefit and profit. Only You ask us to share for our benefit and for our profit. Lord, we ask that You help the surrounding glitter not to blind us, and that You would enlighten us by Your grace, motivate us by Your Spirit, and mature us by Your nature. Amen.

She Did What She Could

Scripture Reading

"While he was in Bethany, reclining at the table in the home of the man known as Simon the Leper, a woman came with an alabaster jar of very expensive perfume, made of pure nard. She broke the jar and broke the perfume on his head" (Mark 14:3).

Meditation

What an extravagant gift. The Scriptures tell us that the woman could have sold the perfume for more than a year's wages. Think of it—your annual salary before deductions put into a bottle, broken, and poured out on Jesus. Some indignantly criticized her and called it a waste. But Jesus said, "She did what she could." Those five words may be five of the grandest words Jesus ever said about anyone concerning his giving. Wouldn't it be wonderful if Jesus could say that about us?

Prayer

Father, thank You for sharing Your extravagant gift with us. Thank You for pouring Your fullness in the body of Jesus and then allowing that body to be broken for us. Lead us to count the cost of not being extravagant. Amen.

Measurements of Living

Scripture Reading

"Command them to do good, to be rich in good deeds, and to be generous and willing to share. In this way they will lay up treasure for themselves as a firm foundation for the coming age, so that they make hold of the life that is truly life" (1 Timothy 6:18, 19).

Meditation

We measure real living not so much by what we drive as by what drives us. Not so much by where we live but who or what lives in us. Not so much by what we make as by what makes us. Not so by what we own as by what owns us. Not so much by our status in the community but by our service in the Kingdom. Not so much by our treasure stored up here but by our treasure stored up in heaven.

Prayer

Father, continue to remind us how fast this age passes away and how quickly we pass through it. May the distance of the coming age draw near our hearts and purpose. Thank You for the promise of coming again for us and of allowing us to inherit Your riches throughout all eternity in Christ. Amen.

Laying It Down

Scripture Reading

"This is how we know what love is: Jesus Christ laid down his life for us. And we ought to lay down our lives for our brothers. If anyone has material possessions and sees his brother in need but has no pity on him, how can the love of God be in him?" (1 John 3:16, 17).

Meditation

When John wrote that we ought to lay down our lives for our brothers, he was not suggesting that we go to a literal cross and have nails pierced through our hands. In the next verse, he talks about sharing our personal possessions with the needy. To lay down our lives means to lay down some of our livelihood for others. Laying down our lives means that we become willing to live more simply so that others may simply live. Only then do we really prove that the love of God is in us—not just in words but also in deeds.

Prayer

O Father, we are overwhelmed with commercials that tempt us to live more sumptuously not simply. Help us to get our thinking straight, our living right, and our giving generous as did Your Son in whose image You have created us. Amen.

More Important Than Giving

Scripture Reading

"'To love him with all your heart, with all your understanding and with all your strength, and to love your neighbor as yourself is more important than all burnt offerings and sacrifices.'

"When Jesus saw that he had answered wisely, he said to him, 'You are not far from the kingdom of God'" (Mark 12:33, 34).

Meditation

Notice that love did not replace burnt offerings and sacrifices, nor did burnt offerings and sacrifices act as a substitute for love. How is loving God and others as ourselves more important than sacrifices? Love motivates giving. Love primes the inside attitude; giving produces the outside action. Love develops the means; giving demonstrates the method. Love creates the motive; giving characterizes the motion. Thus love becomes the channel through which our giving flows to make a difference in peoples' lives. We can see invisible love through visible giving. To say, "we love because He first loved us" also says, "we give because He first gave to us."

Prayer

Father, we cannot deny Your love. Throughout the past You consistently gave to us, and You continue to do so today. With all the treasure You own, thank You for seeing us as the apple of Your eye. Thank You for Your provisions. Help us to allow Your generosity to grow through us. Amen.

An Undivided Heart—Really?

Scripture Reading

"Hear, O Lord, and answer me, for I am poor and needy" (Psalm 86:1).

Meditation

Who was it that said he was poor and needy? It was the King of Judah—David himself. Yet David had houses, stables, closets full of clothes, resources for luxurious feasts, celebrations, holidays, and servants. But with all of that, he said, "I am poor and needy." What did he need? In the rest of that Psalm, he confessed that he needed God's mercy, joy, forgiveness, love, and faithfulness. But David did not just want to receive more from God. He wanted to give more to God, so he asked for an undivided heart. Years later Jesus said, "Where your treasure is, there your heart will be also." An undivided heart costs something.

Prayer

Thank You, Father, for having a heart that abounds in love toward us. Thank You for Your majesty. Make our hearts as undivided for You as Yours is for us. Amen.

God's Plan for Prosperity

Scripture Reading

"One man gives freely, yet gains even more, another withholds unduly, but comes to poverty. A generous man will prosper; he who refreshes will himself be refreshed" (Proverbs 11:24, 25).

Meditation

When will we receive more and what will we receive? We are so impatient; we want the return now. But now is too soon. Someone has observed that anyone can count the seeds in an apple, but only God can count the apples in one seed. Someone can count the dollars in the offering plate, but only God can count the results that these dollars will have locally and around the world. His count will determine the return to us—a return in Heaven. That is better because it is eternal.

Prayer

Thank You, Father, for seeing more benefits to our gift than what our timetable allows us to see. Thank You for what You are laying up for us in Heaven. Amen.

Cultivating Seed

Scripture Reading

"Through these he has given us his very great and precious promises, so that through them you may participate in the divine nature and escape the corruption in the world caused by evil desires" (2 Peter 1:4).

Meditation

God has planted in us His divine nature—the nature of love, of mercy, of patience, of gentleness, of faithfulness, of goodness, of joy, and of peace. It starts in us as a seed. We cultivate the seed of patience by longsuffering. Then the seed of patience grows. We cultivate the seed of gentleness by mellowing our reactions; then that seed grows. We cultivate the seed of kindness by binding our bitter tongues; then the seed of kindness grows. We cultivate the seed of generosity by giving; then that seed grows. God wants the seed of His divine nature to be fully grown in each of us so that we can conform to the image of His Son and have life abundantly.

Prayer

Thank You, Father, for putting the treasure of Yourself in us. Thank You for allowing our bodies to be Your temple, Your vessels, and the recipients of your nature. Increase the desire in us to grow into spiritual maturity. Help us keep our eyes on Jesus.

Index to Part 1

By Scripture and Topic

Special Days **Page**

Index to Part 2

By Scripture and Topic